DESTINATION MARS

INVESTIGATING

MARS

Margaret J. Goldstein

Lerner Publications ◆ Minneapolis

Lerner Publications Company
An imprint of Lerner Publishing Group, Inc.
241 First Avenue North
Minneapolis, MN 55401 USA

For reading levels and more information, look up this title at www.lernerbooks.com.

Main body text set in Aptifer Sans LT Pro.
Typeface provided by Linotype AG.

Library of Congress Cataloging-in-Publication Data

Names: Goldstein, Margaret J., author.
Title: Investigating Mars / Margaret J. Goldstein.
Description: Minneapolis : Lerner Publications, [2024] | Series: Destination Mars (alternator books ®) | Includes bibliographical references and index. | Audience: Ages 8–12 | Audience: Grades 4–6 | Summary: "Are there signs of life on Mars? What is on the Martian surface? Scientists are investigating the planet to find out, and readers can learn about their plans to send up human explorers one day!"— Provided by publisher.
Identifiers: LCCN 2022043074 (print) | LCCN 2022043075 (ebook) | ISBN 9781728490663 (library binding) | ISBN 9798765602768 (paperback) | ISBN 9781728496825 (ebook)
Subjects: LCSH: Mars (Planet)—Juvenile literature.
Classification: LCC QB641 .G6724 2023 (print) | LCC QB641 (ebook) | DDC 523.43—dc23/eng/20220920

LC record available at https://lccn.loc.gov/2022043074
LC ebook record available at https://lccn.loc.gov/2022043075

Manufactured in the United States of America
1-52997-51015-2/3/2023

TABLE OF CONTENTS

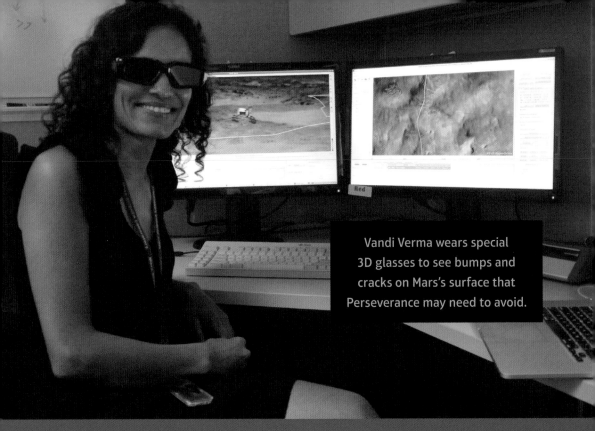

Vandi Verma wears special 3D glasses to see bumps and cracks on Mars's surface that Perseverance may need to avoid.

INTRODUCTION
DRIVING ON MARS

Vandi Verma has one of the coolest jobs in the world. Every day she sits at a computer, puts on 3D glasses, and explores a strange and faraway land. It's like playing a video game. But this is serious work. Verma is an engineer with the National Aeronautics and Space Administration (NASA), the US government's space agency. Her job is to drive the Perseverance rover over the surface of Mars.

Verma drives the rover by remote control. Using radio signals, she tells the rover where to turn and how far to drive. She makes sure it doesn't bump into boulders or fall down hills. Sometimes she tells the rover to do tasks with its robotic arm. The arm contains cameras for taking pictures, drills for digging into the soil, and other equipment.

Perseverance has been exploring Mars since February 2021. It has an exciting mission: to search for signs of ancient life on Mars. Perseverance is not alone on Mars. Two other rovers and a lander are also studying the planet. Eight orbiters circle the planet in space, much like how satellites orbit Earth.

Back on Earth, space agencies from around the world are planning to send more missions to Mars. Someday, humans might investigate Mars in person.

Perseverance carries multiple cameras. One of its cameras captured this selfie of the rover's robotic arm.

Scientists believe Mars and Earth have some similarities.

CHAPTER 1

RED AND ROCKY

Mars is one of eight planets in our solar system. It is about half the size of Earth. Mars, along with the rest of the solar system, formed about 4.6 billion years ago. It is the fourth-closest planet to the sun. It has two moons, Phobos and Deimos.

Deep inside, Mars has a core of molten, or melted, rock. The core is surrounded by a layer of harder, cooler rock. The planet's crust, or outer layer, is also rock. It is red because it contains a lot of iron. This color gives Mars its nickname: the Red Planet.

Over billions of years, many meteoroids and asteroids have smashed into Mars. They made millions of craters on the Martian surface. Mars also has volcanoes. When Mars was a younger planet, hot rock and gases shot up through its

Deep within Mars's interior is a molten core, much like the core within Earth.

volcanoes. The largest volcano, Olympus Mons, towers 16 miles (25 km) into the air.

The Martian atmosphere is made mostly of carbon dioxide. The atmosphere is very thin, which means that gas particles there are spread far apart. Heat and moisture easily escape through the thin atmosphere, so Mars is dry and extremely cold. The average temperature is −80°F (−62°C), but sometimes Mars can be as cold as −200°F (−129°C). The warmest temperature ever recorded on Mars was only 70°F (21°C).

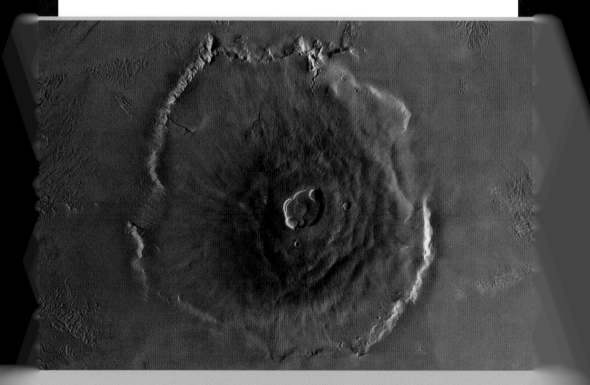

Olympus Mons is one of the tallest mountains in the entire solar system.
It is over two times as tall as Mount Everest.

The astronomer Percival Lowell used his telescope to observe Mars.

THE FIRST MARS MISSIONS

Mars is one of our nearest neighbors in space. Humans have been interested in Mars for thousands of years. In ancient times, people could only see the planet in the night sky. Later, people viewed the Martian surface with telescopes.

In the 1960s, the United States and a former country called the Soviet Union tried to send spacecraft to Mars. Many missions failed. Some spacecraft broke down on the launchpad or out in space. Others crashed into Mars.

Mariner 9 operated for over a year, taking measurements of Mars.
Though it no longer works, it continues to orbit the Red Planet.

In the 1970s, spacecraft finally reached Mars. In 1971, the US craft Mariner 9 became the first spacecraft to orbit Mars, and Mars 3 from the Soviet Union was the first successful lander on Mars. Shortly after landing, Mars 3 stopped working. The first craft to explore Mars from its surface were Viking 1 and 2, from the United States. Mars missions from many countries followed.

The first spacecraft that visited Mars did different jobs. Orbiters took photographs of Mars, studied the planet's gravity, tested gases in the Martian atmosphere, and searched for signs of water. Landers took close-up photographs of the planet's surface and looked for chemicals in the Martian soil. Using radio communications, the spacecraft sent images and other information back to scientists on Earth.

The Spirit rover found volcanic rocks on Mars, showing scientists that Mars used to have volcanoes.

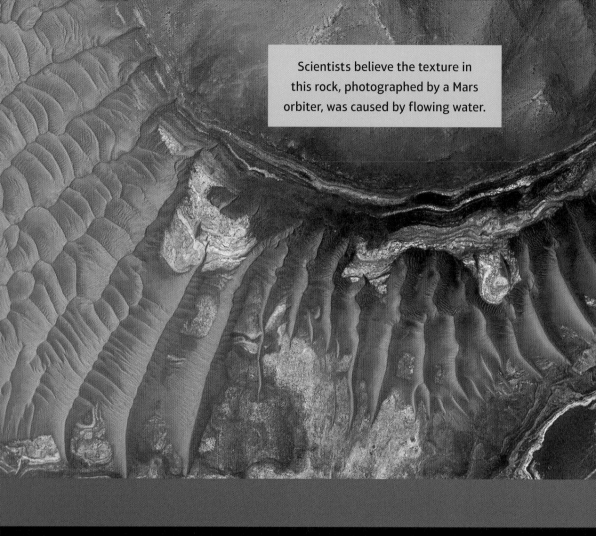

Scientists believe the texture in this rock, photographed by a Mars orbiter, was caused by flowing water.

CHAPTER 2
WATER ON MARS

Mariner 9 took more than seven thousand photographs of Mars and its moons. Some pictures showed Martian volcanoes and craters. Other pictures showed places that looked like empty rivers, streams, and lakes. Scientists suspect that when Mars was young, these places were filled with water.

By studying photos and other information, scientists have devised theories about early Mars. They believe that more than four billion years ago, Mars was much warmer. It had lots of liquid water and a thick atmosphere. So what happened?

Based on data collected from rovers and orbiters, scientists believe Mars once had a huge saltwater ocean.

The solar wind is made of particles flowing out of the sun.

Over time, the solar wind likely blew away much of Mars's atmosphere. Without a thick atmosphere to hold the sun's heat, the planet got colder. Some of its water even froze into ice. Other water turned to gas and drifted off into space.

Mars still has some water, but it is in the form of ice at the planet's north and south poles. Water ice is also underground and mixed in with the Martian soil and rock.

BRINGING MARS TO EARTH

Scientists want to study Martian rocks and soil up close. A mission called Mars Sample Return will make this possible. Designed by NASA and the European Space Agency (ESA), the mission will send vehicles to pick up samples collected by Perseverance and fly them back to Earth. The launch is planned for the late 2020s, with the first samples arriving on Earth in 2033.

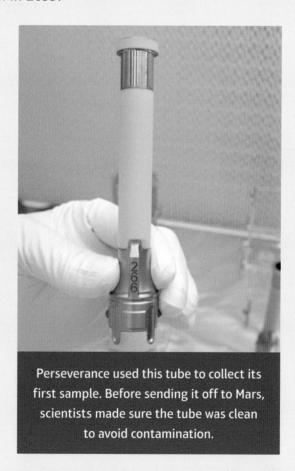

Perseverance used this tube to collect its first sample. Before sending it off to Mars, scientists made sure the tube was clean to avoid contamination.

RECIPE FOR LIFE

So far, Earth is the only planet known to have living things. Earth has many ingredients for life, including water, warm temperatures, and a thick atmosphere. More than four billion years ago, Mars was warm and watery too. It also had a thick atmosphere. Was it home to life then?

Mars contains the solar system's largest canyon, which is full of grooves and layers created by ancient water.

Fossils of microbes are so small that you need special tools to see them.

If Mars once had living things, they probably weren't plants or animals. More likely, they were tiny creatures called microbes. They might have left traces in the Martian soil, such as certain chemicals and gases. They might have even left fossils. Scientists look for these traces when they study soil samples collected by Mars rovers.

Together, the rover Perseverance and the helicopter Ingenuity make a great exploration team.

CHAPTER 3
THE TEAM ON MARS

Many vehicles are at work on Mars. Perseverance digs up soil and rock samples. It carries high-tech instruments that look for water, chemicals, and gases in the samples. The instruments help search for signs of ancient Martian life.

Perseverance also carries a small helicopter, Ingenuity. Standing 1.6 feet (0.5 m) tall and weighing just 4 pounds (1.8 kg), Ingenuity has made dozens of short flights over the Martian surface. Ingenuity will pave the way for more helicopters to visit Mars. Mission planners might use the helicopters to survey the land from above, to visit places that are too steep for rovers, or to carry scientific instruments from one spot to another.

Ingenuity can even take pictures of its own shadow on Mars's surface.

Zhurong is one of many Martian spacecraft from countries other than the United States.

Zhurong, a rover from China, uses radar to study the Martian interior. It looks for ice, liquid water, and signs of ancient life. InSight, a NASA lander, is another recent member of the Mars team. It studied heat and movement deep inside Mars. It lost power in late 2022 due to dust on Mars covering its solar panels, but before that, it detected Marsquakes (the Martian version of earthquakes).

The InSight lander used a sensitive probe to take measurements from within Mars's crust before it lost power in late 2022.

Curiosity, another NASA rover, has been on Mars since 2012. Like Perseverance and Zhurong, Curiosity looks for signs of life.

Curiosity was meant to run only two years, but it has operated for more than ten years.

In addition to the spacecraft sent from Earth, two moons orbit Mars: Phobos and Deimos.

FULL CIRCLE

Orbiters perform a variety of tasks as they circle Mars. Hope, an orbiter from the United Arab Emirates, studies Mars's weather. Mars Express, from the ESA, studies ice at the Martian South Pole. In 2018, Mars Express detected an unusual shape under the ice. Many scientists believe the shape is a lake of liquid water. Mars Express has also traveled close to the moon Phobos. Other orbiters map Mars's atmosphere, take pictures of Mars using high-powered cameras, or send communication signals between Mars and Earth.

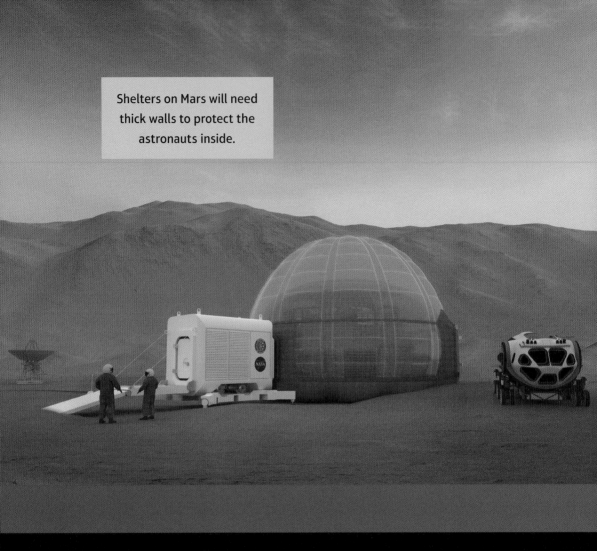

Shelters on Mars will need thick walls to protect the astronauts inside.

CHAPTER 4

HUMAN INVESTIGATORS

Space agencies hope to one day send human travelers to Mars. These astronauts will be able to study Martian rocks, soil, and water at laboratories on Mars. Humans on Mars will hear the Martian wind and smell sulfur from ancient volcanoes. These sensations will provide more information for scientific study.

Sometimes, rovers get stuck in sand or at the bottom of steep Martian slopes. Exploring on foot, humans might be better able to navigate the rugged Martian terrain. Astronauts will also work together with rovers, landers, helicopters, and scientific instruments. They'll be able to fix broken machines and drive rovers over the Martian surface. They will communicate with mission controllers on Earth as they work.

Mission controllers are scientists who make sure everything in a space mission goes according to plan.

Astronauts have successfully grown food aboard the International Space Station, which orbits Earth.

HOME AWAY FROM HOME

Space agencies hope to send astronauts to Mars in the 2030s or 2040s. The mission will be complicated. It will involve a long space journey, lasting at least six months each way. After reaching Mars, astronauts might live at an orbiting base camp. From there, they would descend to the Martian surface to study it up close.

On each step of the trip, astronauts will need supplies of oxygen, food, water, and fuel. They will also need protection from deadly radiation and extreme cold. On the surface of Mars, they will need space suits and shelters to keep them warm and safe. Mission planners are figuring out how to meet these needs. For example, robots might build shelters before astronauts arrive on Mars. A machine called the Mars Oxygen In-Situ Resource Utilization Experiment (MOXIE) might create extra oxygen for astronauts to breathe. Other machines might extract drinking water from the Martian soil. Astronauts might grow their own food in greenhouses.

Greenhouses on Mars will need walls and windows that can protect food inside from the planet's dangerous environment.

MOXIE

Perseverance carried MOXIE to Mars. This device converts carbon dioxide from the Martian atmosphere into oxygen. MOXIE has so far created only small amounts of oxygen. NASA wants to use the technology to make much larger amounts. Someday, astronauts might use the oxygen as breathable air and as fuel for space vehicles.

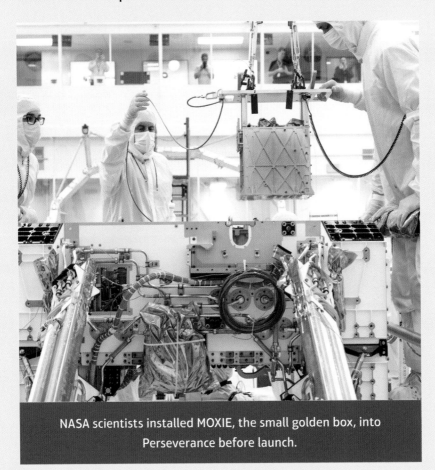

NASA scientists installed MOXIE, the small golden box, into Perseverance before launch.

THE PLAN FOR RETURNING SAMPLES TO EARTH

1. PERSEVERANCE PUTS SAMPLES IN SEALED TUBES.

2. ANOTHER ROVER PICKS UP TUBES AND TAKES THEM TO A LANDER WITH A SMALL ROCKET.

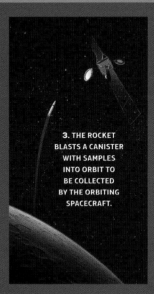

3. THE ROCKET BLASTS A CANISTER WITH SAMPLES INTO ORBIT TO BE COLLECTED BY THE ORBITING SPACECRAFT.

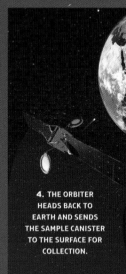

4. THE ORBITER HEADS BACK TO EARTH AND SENDS THE SAMPLE CANISTER TO THE SURFACE FOR COLLECTION.

BACK TO EARTH

After spending several months on Mars, astronauts will head home. They'll need an ascent vehicle to carry them through the Martian atmosphere. It will take them back to the orbiting base camp. From there, astronauts will board another craft for the trip back to Earth.

From start to finish, a human journey to Mars won't be easy. For the astronauts, it might be dangerous, lonely, and scary. But the mission will also be exciting for everyone. It will help us learn much more about our near neighbor in space.

Glossary

atmosphere: a layer of gases surrounding a planet

fossil: an impression of an ancient organism left in rock or an ancient organism whose remains have turned to rock

gravity: a force that pulls objects toward the surface of a planet, sun, or other space object. Gravity also attracts objects in space to one another.

lander: a spacecraft that lands on the surface of a planet or moon

orbiter: a spacecraft that circles a planet or another body in space

radar: a system for analyzing the movement or makeup of objects by bouncing radio waves off them

radiation: powerful energy that travels through space and can be deadly to living things

robotic arm: a section of a robot that functions much like a human arm. It can grasp and move objects and operate machinery.

rover: a wheeled vehicle equipped with cameras and other instruments, designed to explore the surface of a planet

solar system: the sun and everything that travels around it, including planets, asteroids, and moons

solar wind: a stream of particles emitted by the sun

theory: an idea intended to explain something or answer questions

water ice: the term astronomers use for frozen water

Learn More

Chapman, Ty. *Mars Rovers*. Minneapolis: Lerner Publications, 2024.

Facts about Mars
https://www.natgeokids.com/uk/discover/science/space/facts
-about-mars/

Hirsch, Rebecca E. *Space Machines in Action*. Minneapolis: Lerner Publications, 2020.

Hubbard, Ben. *The Story of Mars*. London: Franklin Watts, 2020.

Kenney, Karen Latchana. *Breakthroughs in Mars Exploration*. Minneapolis: Lerner Publications, 2019.

Mars Facts for Kids
https://nineplanets.org/kids/mars/

Mars Missions—Rovers
https://www.planetsforkids.org/missions/mars-missions-rovers.html

Space Place: Solar System
https://spaceplace.nasa.gov/menu/solar-system/

Index

Photo Acknowledgments

Image credits: NASA/JPL-Caltech, pp. 4, 5, 15, 18, 19, 28; BT Image/Shutterstock,
p. 6; AlexLMX/Getty Images, p. 7; NASA/JPL/USGS, p. 8; Chronicle/Alamy Stock
Photo, p. 9; NASA/JPL, pp. 10, 12; NASA/JPL-Caltech/Cornell/NMMNH, p. 11; NASA/
GSFC, p. 13; john finney photography/Getty Images, p. 14; NASA/JPL-Caltech/Univ.
of Arizona, p. 16; FrentaN/Shutterstock, p. 17; -/CNS/CNSA/AFP/Getty Images,
p. 20; B.A.E. Inc./Alamy Stock Photo, p. 21; NASA, pp. 22, 26; Elena11/Shutterstock,
p. 23; NASA/Clouds AO/SEArch, p. 24; NASA/Ames, p. 25; Vac1/Shutterstock, p. 27;
The Planetary Society/Wikimedia Commons (CC BY 3.0), p. 29.

Cover: MARK GARLICK/SCIENCE PHOTO LIBRARY/Getty Images.